FEB 0 1 2008

P9-CJK-563

NAPA CITY-COUNTY LIBRARY
580 COOMBS STREET
NAPA CA 94559-3396

Family Trees

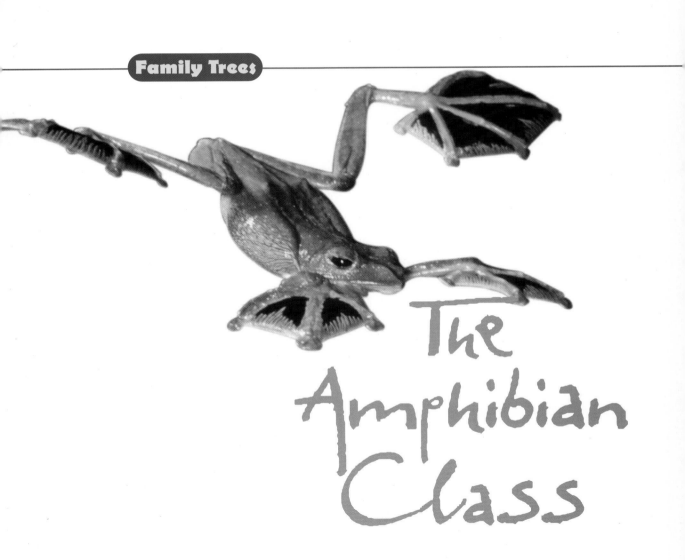

The Amphibian Class

R E B E C C A   S T E F O F F

Marshall Cavendish
Benchmark
New York

With thanks to Dan Wharton, Ph.D., Director, Central Park Zoo, for his expert review of the manuscript.

Marshall Cavendish Benchmark
99 White Plains Road
Tarrytown, New York 10591-9001
www.marshallcavendish.us
Text copyright © 2008 by Rebecca Stefoff
Illustrations copyright © 2008 by Marshall Cavendish Corporation
Illustrations by Robert Romagnoli

All rights reserved. No part of this book may be reproduced or utilized in any form or by any means electronic or mechanical including photocopying, recording, or by any information storage and retrieval system, without permission from the copyright holders.

All Web sites were available and accurate when this book was sent to press.

Editor: Karen Ang
Publisher: Michelle Bisson
Art Director: Anahid Hamparian
Series Designer: Patrice Sheridan

Library of Congress Cataloging-in-Publication Data
Stefoff, Rebecca, date
The Amphibian class / by Rebecca Stefoff.
p. cm. -- (Family trees)
Summary: "Explores the habitats, life cycles, and other characteristics of animals in the Amphibian class"--Provided by publisher.
Includes bibliographical references and index.
ISBN 978-0-7614-2692-9
1. Amphibians--Juvenile literature. I. Title. II. Series.

QL644.2.S742 2007
597.8--dc22

2007003487

Front cover: Chachi tree frogs
Title page: Wallace's flying frog
Back cover: An axolotl

Photo Research by Candlepants Incorporated
Cover Photo: Pete Oxford / Minden Pictures
The photographs in this book are used by permission and through the courtesy of:
Animals Animals: Stephen Dalton, 3, 41; OSF/Stephen Dalton, 6; Zig Lesczcynski, 11, 70; E. R. Degginger, 17, 30, 61; David M. Dennis, 22; Breck P. Kent, 32; Michael Fogden, 46, 72; Raymond Mendez, 51, 63; Paul Freed, 73; Allen Blake Sheldon, 77, 83. *Photo Researchers Inc.:* Pascal Goetgheluck, 12; Tom McHugh, 29, 66; Valerie Giles, 44; Stephen Dalton, 45, 59, back cover; Mark Smith, 71, 74; Art Wolfe, 86. *Corbis:* Jonathan Blair, 16, 20; Joe McDonald, 25. *National Science Foundation:* Zina Deretsky, 19. *Minden Pictures:* Pete Oxford, 23, 42; Stephen Dalton, 26; Mitsuhiko Imamori, 31; Michael & Patricia Fogden, 33, 36, 39, 69; Mark Moffett, 34, 35, 82; Piotr Naskrecki, 38, 68; Heidi & Hans-Jurgen Koch, 47, 78; Frans Lanting, 50; Rene Krekels/Foto Natura, 54, 57; ZSSD, 76; Hugo Willocx/Foto Natura, 79. *Saravanakumar/ecotone:* S.U. Saravanakumar, 49. *The Bridgeman Art Library:* Archives Charmet, Bibliotheque des Arts Decoratifs, Paris, France, 52. *Visuals Unlimited:* Gary Meszaros, 53; Ken Lucas, 58; Jack Dermid, 62. *Timothy R. Burkhardt:* 7, 65. *Peter Arnold Inc.:* John Cancalosi, 84.

Printed in Malaysia
1 3 5 6 4 2

CONTENTS

A leopard frog leaping into a pond showcases the amphibian's ability to be at home in two worlds.

Classifying Life

"There is a frog called the Land-frog," an unknown author wrote in the second century CE, in a book called the *Physiologus*. The Land-frog can live "in the heat and the glow of the sun, but when the rain touches him he dies." Another animal called the Water-frog hates heat and light so much that if "the sun's ray touches it, immediately it dives under the water again."

Whoever wrote the *Physiologus* knew more folklore than fact. There is no "Land-frog" that is killed by rain—although many kinds of frogs can be found on land and in the water. In fact, the combination of land and water makes a frog what it is: an amphibian.

"Amphibian" comes from the Greek words *amphi* (meaning "double") and *bios* (meaning "life"). Like a car that turns into a boat when driven into a lake, or a raft that becomes a truck when it reaches shore, a frog is at home in two worlds, the water and the land. Frogs and their close relatives belong to a class of animals called amphibians because their lives are spent partly in water and partly on land. To understand their place in the animal kingdom, it helps to know something about how scientists classify living things.

THE INVENTION OF TAXONOMY

Science provides tools for making sense of the natural world. One of the most powerful tools is classification, which means organizing things in a pattern according to their differences and similarities. Since ancient times, scientists who study plants and animals have been developing taxonomy, a classification system for living things. Taxonomy groups together plants or animals that share certain features, and sets them apart from other plants and animals with different features.

Taxonomy is hierarchical, which means that it is arranged in levels of categories. The highest levels include many kinds of organisms. These large categories are divided into smaller ones, which in turn are divided into still smaller ones. The smallest formal category of all is the species, a single kind of organism. The idea behind taxonomy is simple, but the world of living things is complex and full of surprises. Taxonomy is not a fixed pattern. It keeps changing to reflect new knowledge or ideas. Over time, scientists have developed rules for adjusting that pattern even when they disagree on its details.

One of the first taxonomists was the ancient Greek philosopher Aristotle (384-322 BCE), who investigated many branches of science, including biology. Aristotle arranged living things on a sort of ladder, or scale. At the bottom were those he considered lowest, or least developed, such as worms. Above them were things he considered higher, or more developed, such as fish, then birds, then mammals.

For centuries after Aristotle, taxonomy made little progress. People who studied nature tended to group organisms together by obvious features, such as separating trees from grasses or birds from fish. However, they did not try to develop a system for classifying all life. Then, between 1682 and 1705, an English naturalist named John Ray published a plan of the living world that was designed to have a place for every species of plant and animal. Ray's system was hierarchical, with several levels of larger and smaller categories. It was the foundation of modern taxonomy.

Swedish naturalist Carolus Linnaeus (1707-1778) built on that foundation to create the taxonomic system used today. Linnaeus was chiefly interested in plants, but his system of classification included all living things. The highest level of classification was the kingdom. To Linnaeus, everything belonged to either the plant or the animal kingdom. Each of these kingdoms was divided into a number of smaller categories called classes. Each class was divided into orders. Each order was divided into genera. Each genus (the singular form of genera) contained one or more species.

Linnaeus also developed another of Ray's ideas, a method for naming species. Before Linnaeus published his important work *System of Nature* in 1735, scientists had no recognized system for referring to plants and animals. Organisms were generally known by their common names, but many of them had different names in different countries. As a result, naturalists often called the same plant or animal by different names. Sometimes they used the same name to refer to different organisms. Linnaeus wanted to end such confusion and allow scholars everywhere to communicate clearly when writing about plants and animals. He established the practice of giving each plant or animal a two-part scientific name consisting of its genus and species, both in Latin, which was the scientific language of Linnaeus's day. The African clawed toad whose common name is the platanna, for example, has the scientific name *Xenopus laevis* (or *X. laevis* after the first time the full name is used). This amphibian belongs to the genus *Xenopus*, which includes other kinds of African clawed toads. The second part of the name, *laevis*, refers only to the platanna.

Linnaeus named hundreds of species. Other scientists quickly adopted his highly flexible system to name thousands more. The Linnaean system appeared at a time when European naturalists were exploring the rest of the world, finding thousands of new plants and animals. This flood of discoveries was overwhelming at times, but Linnaean taxonomy helped scientists identify and organize their finds for systematic study.

TAXONOMY TODAY

Biologists still use the system of scientific naming that Linnaeus developed (anyone who discovers a new species can choose its scientific name, which must be in Latin). Other aspects of taxonomy, though, have changed since Linnaeus's time.

As biologists learned more about living things, they added new levels to taxonomy to reflect their growing understanding of the similarities and differences among organisms. Eventually, an organism's full classification could include the following taxonomic levels: kingdom, subkingdom, phylum (for animals) or division (sometimes used for plants and fungi), subphylum or subdivision, superclass, class, subclass, infraclass, order, superfamily, family, genus, species, and subspecies or variety.

Another change concerned the kinds of information that scientists use to classify organisms. The earliest naturalists used obvious physical features, such as the differences between reptiles and mammals, to divide organisms into general groups. By the time of Ray and Linnaeus, naturalists could study specimens in more detail. Aided by new tools such as the microscope, they explored the inner structures of plants and animals. For a long time after Linnaeus, classification was based mainly on details of anatomy, or physical structure, although scientists also looked at how an organism reproduced and how and where it lived.

Biologists can now peer more deeply into an organism's inner workings than Aristotle or Linnaeus ever dreamed possible. They can look inside its individual cells and study the arrangement of DNA that makes up its genetic blueprint. Genetic information is key to modern classification because DNA is more than an organism's blueprint—it also contains clues to how closely that organism is related to other species and how long ago those species separated during the process of evolution.

In recent years, many biologists have pointed out that the Linnaean system is a patchwork of old and new ideas. It doesn't clearly reflect the latest knowledge about evolutionary connections among organisms both living and extinct. Some

Classification of the Argentine Horned Frog

It's round and has a big mouth, but it's not the gobbling blob from the 1980s arcade game Pac-Man. It's the Argentine horned frog, also called the South American ornate frog. Its scientific classification shows the various levels of taxonomy:

Kingdom:	Animalia (animals)
Phylum:	Chordata (with spinal chords)
Subphylum:	Vertebrata (with segmented backbones)
Class:	Amphibia (water and land life cycle, undergo metamorphosis)
Subclass:	Lissamphibia (not extinct)
Order:	Anura (frogs and toads)
Family:	Ceratophryidae (horned)
Subfamily:	Ceratophryinae
Genus:	*Ceratophrys*
Species:	*ornate*

scientists now call for a new approach to taxonomy, one based entirely on evolutionary relationships. One of the most useful new approaches is called phylogenetics, or cladistics. This method groups together all organisms that are descended from the same ancestor. Scientists arrange organisms in branching, treelike diagrams called cladograms. These show the order in which groups of plants or animals split off from a line of shared ancestry.

None of the proposed new systems of classifying living things has yet been agreed upon by all scientists. Most experts recognize the importance of cladistics while still using the two main features of Linnaean taxonomy: the hierarchy of categories and the two-part species name. Yet scientists may disagree about the proper term for a category, or hold conflicting views about the classification of a particular plant or animal. Experts often debate whether two organisms belong to the same species or to different species, or whether an organism represents a new species.

Even at the highest level of classification, not all scientists agree on a single, final taxonomy. A few of them still divide all life into two kingdoms, plants and animals. Others divide life into as many as thirteen kingdoms. Most scientists, though, use systems of classification that have five or six kingdoms: plants, animals, fungi, and two or three kingdoms of microscopic organisms such as bacteria, amoebas, and algae.

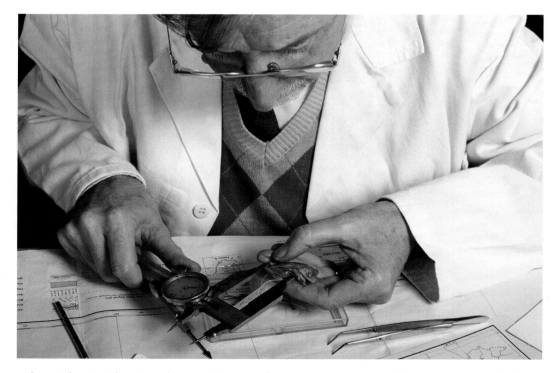

A herpetologist at the Natural History Museum of Paris measures a newly discovered tree frog in the genus *Hyla*. The measurements will become part of the scientific description of the species.

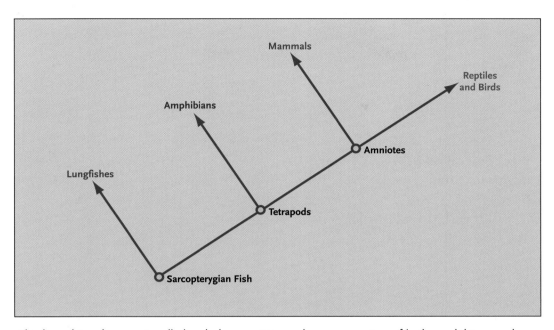

This branching diagram is called a cladogram. Tetrapods were ancestors of both amphibians and amniotes (animals whose embroyos develop inside fluid-filled membranes).

Plant and animal classifications change often as scientists apply new evolutionary or genetic insights to taxonomy. In recent years, such insights have caused herpetologists—scientists who study amphibians and reptiles—to move amphibians into different categories and even to rearrange the categories themselves. Fieldwork in ponds and forests around the world, together with laboratory research, is bringing constant change to the centuries-old science of classifying living things.

Scientists classify living things in arrangements like this family tree of the animal

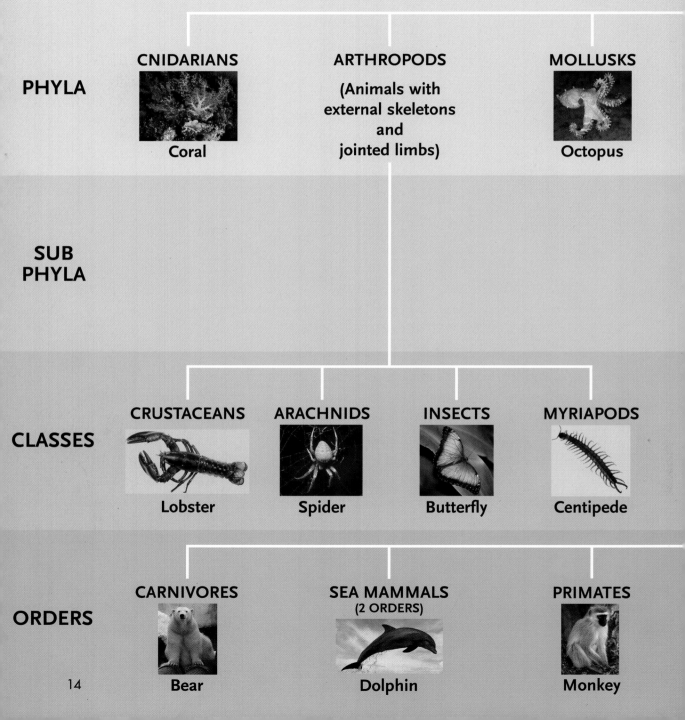

ANIMAL

PHYLA

CNIDARIANS

Coral

ARTHROPODS

(Animals with external skeletons and jointed limbs)

MOLLUSKS

Octopus

SUB PHYLA

CLASSES

CRUSTACEANS

Lobster

ARACHNIDS

Spider

INSECTS

Butterfly

MYRIAPODS

Centipede

ORDERS

CARNIVORES

Bear

SEA MAMMALS
(2 ORDERS)

Dolphin

PRIMATES

Monkey

kingdom to highlight the connections and the differences among the many forms of life.

KINGDOM

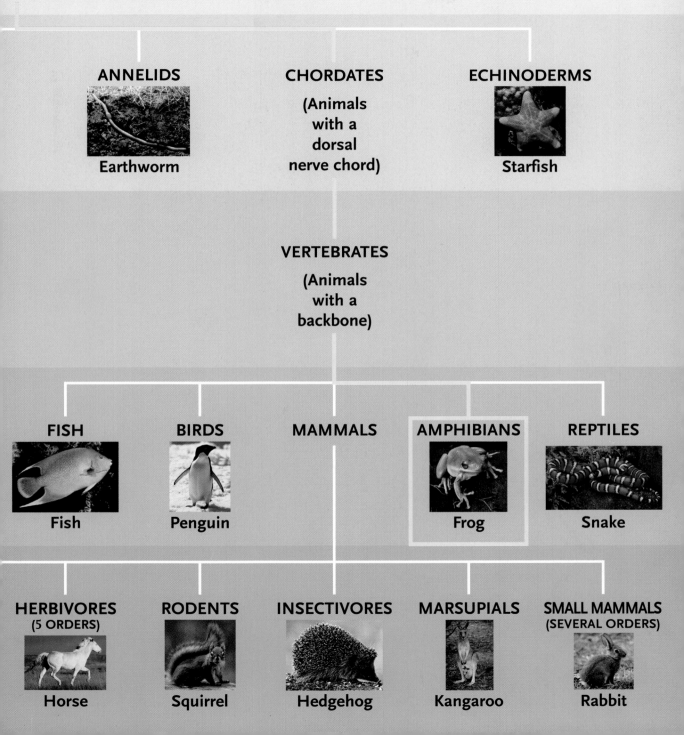

ANNELIDS

Earthworm

CHORDATES

(Animals with a dorsal nerve chord)

ECHINODERMS

Starfish

VERTEBRATES

(Animals with a backbone)

FISH

Fish

BIRDS

Penguin

MAMMALS

AMPHIBIANS

Frog

REPTILES

Snake

HERBIVORES
(5 ORDERS)

Horse

RODENTS

Squirrel

INSECTIVORES

Hedgehog

MARSUPIALS

Kangaroo

SMALL MAMMALS
(SEVERAL ORDERS)

Rabbit

A frog fossil unearthed in Germany has preserved not just the animal's skeleton but some of its tissues as well, such as the webbing between its toes. Although the fossil is forty-nine million years old, this frog had many of the features seen in frogs and toads today.

Amphibians Yesterday and Today

Amphibians have been around for longer than 230 million years—probably much longer, although scientists don't know exactly when they first appeared. The dawn of the amphibians is one of the biggest mysteries in paleontology, the study of early life-forms. But paleontologists do know that amphibians were among the first descendants of pioneering creatures called tetrapods, fishlike animals that left the sea to try life on land.

As amphibians evolved over the ages, many species became extinct, but new ones developed. Today amphibians range from the brilliantly colored poison frogs of the Amazon rain forest to the seldom-seen caecilians, which look like enormous earthworms. Amphibians live on every continent except Antarctica. Their habitats include underground rivers, rocky mountain slopes, boggy meadows, and more. Scientists are still discovering new species of these ancient, adaptable survivors.

FOUR-LEGGED ORIGINS

For a long time, biology textbooks said that amphibians evolved from fish and were the first animals to venture onto land. Reptiles, in turn, evolved from amphibians. For this reason, some older books suggested that reptiles are a "higher" form of life, while amphibians are "lower," or more primitive.

The real story of amphibian evolution, scientists now know, is more complicated. It started sometime between 416 and 359 million years ago, in an era that paleontologists call the Devonian Period. The seas were full of vertebrates, or animals with backbones. All of those animals were fish, but there were many kinds. One group of fish had bony skeletons and supporting structures made of bone within their fins. Paleontologists call these fish the Sarcopterygii, or sarcopterygian fish. They had lungs. Some of them even had nostrils so that they could breathe with their mouths closed, or when their mouths were underwater but their nostrils were above the surface. These features—bony fins that could develop into legs, and air-breathing lungs—made the sarcopterygians good candidates to evolve into land animals.

How and why did fish first move onto the land? Once, scientists believed that severe droughts led to this milestone in evolution. As pools and ponds dried up, fish used their fins to flop across the land in search of larger bodies of water. The survivors spent longer and longer on land. Eventually their fins evolved into feet, and they became the early four-legged land animals known as tetrapods.

Recent studies, however, don't support the idea that the Devonian Period had frequent droughts. Now scientists think that the shift from water to land happened *after* some fish developed legs. In 2005 scientists working in the North American Arctic discovered the fossil of a creature partway between a fish and a tetrapod. Called *Tiktaalik*, it lived about 385 million years ago. It had a neck—found in tetrapods but not in fish—and its limbs combined features of a fish's fins and a tetrapod's legs.

Tiktaalik, which lived about 385 million years ago, was a link between fish and four-legged animals. The bones of its front fins correspond to the shoulder, arm, elbow, and wrist bones of land-dwellers.

The first true four-legged animals probably evolved from *Tiktaalik,* or creatures like it, and lived in shallow water. They used their legs as paddles for swimming, supporting their weight on muddy lake bottoms, or pushing their way through reeds and other water vegetation. Later, their legs grew strong enough to support the weight of their bodies. Around 360 million years ago, these tetrapods began going onto the land. Maybe they went to escape predators who hunted in the water. Another possibility is that the land offered new food sources, such as insects.

The early tetrapods evolved into a wide variety of forms. Some had gills and lived in the water, at least part of the time. Others spent more time on land. A few species were quite large. *Mastodonsaurus,* which lived during the Triassic Period from 248 to 205 million years ago, measured about 13 feet (4 meters) in length, the size of a large modern alligator.

The early tetrapods are often called amphibians, and they had some of the physical features of modern amphibians. Yet the link between the early tetrapods and modern amphibians is unclear. Scientists know from fossil evidence that reptiles evolved from the tetrapods, splitting off from them around 320 million years ago (eventually, birds and mammals evolved from the reptiles). But there is a big gap in the fossil record between the ancient amphibious tetrapods and the line of amphibians that leads directly to modern species. For this reason, the evolution from tetrapods into the ancestors

Another ancient fossil, *Acanthostega gunnari,* has features of both fish and amphibians. Some scientists now think that creatures like this developed legs before they migrated onto land.

of modern species is a mystery. Herpetologist Kraig Adler calls it "the biggest fossil gap in the history of terrestrial vertebrates" (land-dwelling animals with backbones).

THE LISSAMPHIBIA

In traditional taxonomy, the Class Amphibia includes all of the amphibian species alive today, as well as extinct species that were directly related to them. In cladistic taxonomy, Amphibia refers to the last common ancestor of all amphibians alive today (even though scientists don't yet know what that ancestor was) and all of its descendants, extinct or alive. Some experts now use the name Lissamphibia for a subclass that includes only living species and their immediate ancestors. This avoids confusion with broader definitions of Amphibia that might include the early tetrapod amphibians.

Most herpetologists and paleontologists now agree that all modern amphibians are descended from the same ancestor, although there is disagreement about which family of ancient tetrapods that ancestor belonged to. A few experts, however, think that caecilians may have evolved from a different ancestor than frogs and salamanders. Either way, ever since the Jurassic Period, which ended about 144 million years ago, the amphibian class has had three subgroups, called orders.

All three orders have multiple names. That's because scientists adopt new names for taxonomic categories slowly—and some never adopt them at all. In the case of amphibians, several new names have come into use in recent years. An order of amphibians might have one name in an encyclopedia and a different name in an article in a scientific magazine.

The three orders of amphibians are Anura, the frogs and toads (this order is sometimes called Salientia); Caudata, the salamanders and newts (this order was formerly called Urodela); and Gymnophiona, the caecilians (sometimes called Apoda). Some taxonomists group Anura and Caudata together in a superorder called Batrachia, because frogs and salamanders have more in common with each other than either group has with caecilians.

The oldest known fossil of an amphibian that is clearly related to modern species is 230 million years old. It is a froglike creature called *Triadobatrachus,* found on the African island of Madagascar. Another froglike fossil, almost as old, comes from Poland. *Eocaecilia,* the oldest fossil ancestor of the caecilians, was found in Arizona. It dates from about 190 million years ago. The earliest known salamander is *Marmorerepton,* which lived in the rivers and streams of Britain 165 million years ago.

Triadobatrachus, Eocaecilia, and *Marmorerepton* died out ages ago, and thousands of other amphibian species became extinct over the years. About six thousand species exist today, making amphibians the second smallest class of living vertebrates, after mammals.

CREATURES' FEATURES

The subclass name Lissamphibia focuses on a distinctive feature of modern amphibians—their skin. The prefix *liss-* means "smooth." Amphibians have no scales, feathers, or fur. Although some have rough or bumpy skins, most are smooth and moist.

An amphibian's skin serves many purposes. Depending upon the species, the skin contains various kinds of small organs called glands. Mucous glands produce moisture that protects and lubricates the skin. Hedonic glands produce chemicals called pheromones that help the animal attract mates. Finally, parotoid and granular glands help defend amphibians from predators by producing toxins, or poisons. The mild versions of these chemicals simply give the animals an unpleasant taste. The strongest versions are powerful enough to kill large predators, including people.

The brilliant coloring of some amphibians, such as this barred tiger salamander, can function as a "Keep Off" sign. It warns potential predators of an unpleasant—or even poisonous—taste.

The Lake Titicaca frog lives in a lake high in the Andes Mountains of South America. The water is low in oxygen, but the frog's baggy, folded skin gives extra surface area for cutaneous respiration, or breathing through the skin.

In amphibians as in some other kinds of animals, special skin cells called chromatophores control skin color. Not all amphibians change color, but many do. Some changes occur slowly, with the changing seasons or the stages of life. Other color changes happen in just seconds. They are meant to help the animal blend into its surroundings, scare off a potential predator, or attract a mate.

The skin of an amphibian is permeable, which means that water and gases can pass through it. In a process called gas exchange, oxygen enters the blood vessels, and carbon dioxide leaves them, through microscopic openings in the skin. Although nearly all amphibians have lungs for breathing, they are also capable of cutaneous respiration, or breathing through their skins. Many of them breathe through special areas of their skin during aquatic phases of their lives, or when they are in water. A few species of salamanders, however, have no lungs at all. They rely on cutaneous respiration to survive.

The skin's permeability to water means that amphibians don't need to drink—they get all the water they need just by absorbing moisture from their environments through their skins. But permeability can also cause problems. Amphibians' skins dry out quickly in hot, dry, or windy conditions, which is why amphibians are more active at night than in daytime, and why the greatest concentrations of species are found in damp habitats. Although amphibians like moisture, none lives in a marine environment. Amphibians cannot maintain the right balance of fresh water in their bodies when surrounded by the salty water of the sea. Still, several species of frogs and salamanders can survive high levels of salt for briefs periods of time, and the Southeast Asian crab-eating frog has evolved to live in mangrove swamps, where the water is brackish—a mix of fresh and salt.

Temperature sets another limit on where amphibians can live. Like reptiles, amphibians are ectothermic, or cold-blooded. They do not have metabolisms that maintain steady temperatures within their bodies, as is the case in birds and mammals. Instead, amphibians' body temperatures are determined by the warmth of their environments. This is one reason amphibians don't live in the world's coldest regions: Antarctica, the northern part of the Arctic, and the highest mountaintops.

Amphibians do, however, live on mountains and in climates with harsh winters. Several strategies help these creatures survive cold conditions. Some species burrow into the earth below the level of frost and spend the coldest months in hibernation, a state of greatly reduced activity that conserves energy. A handful of frog and salamander species, including the wood frog and spring peeper of North America, have natural antifreeze. Their blood contains chemicals called glucose and glycerol. These lower the freezing point of blood, keeping it flowing at temperatures that would otherwise freeze the animals to death.

Amphibians are set apart from other animals—even from their close relatives the reptiles—by several unique features of their anatomy, or physical structure. One is a kind of tooth found in no other animal. Scientists call it a pedicellate tooth. It has two parts: a base called a pedicel and a pointed crown that is attached to the pedicel by flexible tissue. The crown of the tooth can bend inward when the amphibian pulls prey into its mouth. If a crown breaks off, another one grows up from inside the pedicel. Another distinctive feature of amphibian anatomy is the levator bulbi, a sheet of muscle beneath the eyes. Its lets the animals raise and lower their

A toad devours a worm, pulling it inward with its teeth. If a tooth breaks, an amphibian can grow a new one.

eyeballs, which can improve their ability to see when they are partly submerged in water or mud.

Not all physical features are shared by all amphibians. Take legs, for example. Amphibians evolved from tetrapods, which got their name because they had four legs. Over the course of evolution, some amphibians lost some or all of their legs. Today there are species with four legs, two legs, and no legs at all. The animals' preferred habitats are varied, too. Although most species spend time both in the water and on land, some are entirely aquatic or entirely terrestrial.

Of all features of amphibian life, the best-known might be metamorphosis—the sudden change from an early stage of growth to an adult. Anyone who has ever watched tadpoles turn into tiny frogs has witnessed metamorphosis. Some insects and other creatures also undergo metamorphosis, but amphibians are the only vertebrates that do it. Metamorphosis happens differently among the three different orders of amphibian life. It is most dramatic among the anurans, or frogs and toads. Widely varied in body type and way of life, the anurans number far more species than either of the other two orders of amphibians.

It's easy to see how *Bombina orientalis* got its common name: the oriental fire-bellied toad. Native to southeastern Siberia, northeastern China, and Korea, these small, active amphibians are also bred for the pet trade.

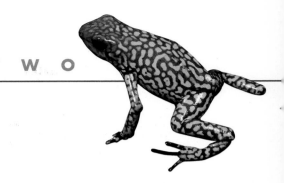

Frogs and Toads

More than 5,300 species of amphibians—about 88 percent of the known amphibians—are anurans. All anurans are four-legged, short-bodied animals without tails. But which are frogs, and which are toads?

To most Europeans and North Americans, anurans with smooth skin and long legs are frogs, while those with rough, warty skin and short, stumpy legs are toads. People in other parts of the world use the terms differently, however, and some herpetologists don't use them at all. They know that every species of anuran can be considered a frog. When scientists do use the term "toad," some of them apply it only to the 250 or so species in the genus *Bufo,* the "true toads." Other scientists continue to use the term when it occurs in the traditional common names of other species.

FAMILIES, FEATURES, AND HABITATS

Taxonomists divide the Order Anura into families, but the number of families varies from one taxonomist to the next. In its online list of amphibian species of the world, the American Museum of Natural History recognizes forty-four anuran families, some of which are divided into subfamilies. The Animal Diversity Web of the University of Michigan's Museum of Zoology, on the other hand, recognizes twenty-five families.

One widely used taxonomic system identifies twenty-eight families of anurans. Each family consists of genera that share features of anatomy and reproduction. A survey of these families reveals the great diversity of the most common amphibians, the frogs.

The family of New Zealand frogs has adapted to life on mountains that have little water. Females lay their eggs in damp soil, and males stick around to tend the eggs. In one species, the male carries the tadpoles on his back. Male midwife toads—species found in Europe and North America—also care for the eggs.

Fire-bellied toads are a family found in many parts of Europe and Asia. Their name comes from the bright red, orange, or yellow markings on

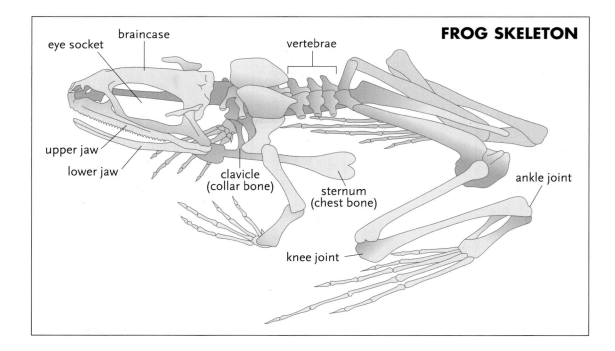

FROG SKELETON

eye socket

braincase

vertebrae

upper jaw

lower jaw

clavicle
(collar bone)

sternum
(chest bone)

knee joint

ankle joint

Megophrys nasuta, the Malayan horned frog, hunts for insects and worms on Southeast Asian forest floors. Its shape and coloring help it blend into the background. From above, it looks like just another leaf.

their underside. As in many amphibian species, these markings are a warning to predators that the animals can be dangerous to eat. The fire-bellied toads spend most of their lives in water, as do their relatives the barbourulas, who live in streams on the Asian islands of Borneo and the Philippines.

Tailed frogs live in North American streams. These few species don't really have tails, but the males have visible organs for mating (unlike most frogs), which can look like tails.

Asian toadfrogs are native to Southeast Asia. Some species, such as the Malayan horned frog, have fleshy spikes or horns near their eyes or mouths. A number of toadfrogs have cryptic coloration, a type of coloring that makes an animal disappear into its background. Brown patches and raised lines in the skin, for example, can make one of these frogs look like a dead leaf lying on the forest floor.

The spadefoot toad family spans Europe, western Asia, and North America. Unlike many amphibians, spadefoot toads thrive in dry, sandy habitats. Their name comes from the fact that they use their hind feet like

The Surinam toad belongs to the pipid family. All members of this family have flat bodies that hug the streambeds and pond bottoms of their habitats.

spades, or shovels, to dig burrows. A growth called a tubercle on the bottom of the foot is tough and sharp enough to cut quickly through soil.

The pipid family of water-dwelling anurans includes clawed frogs and Surinam toads. Pipids have very flat bodies with eyes that point upward, long legs, webbed hind feet, and long fingers on their forelimbs. As they forage on the bottoms of ponds and streams, the pipids use their forelimbs to shovel small fish and aquatic insects into their wide mouths. Surinam toads have an unusual reproductive strategy. After the female lays her eggs, the male uses his feet to brush them onto her back, where they stick. They hatch not into tadpoles but into tiny toadlets that spend three or four months living in small pockets, or hollows, on their mother's back before swimming off to start life on their own.

The widespread Bufonidae family contains several kinds of anurans. The largest belong to the genus *Bufo*, the "true toads," such as *Bufo bufo*, the European common toad. These thick-bodied animals hop or run across the ground, but they cannot leap. The ancient Romans found their

A Japanese toad snatches an insect. Many anurans capture prey by shooting out a long, sticky tongue, then pulling it back into the mouth with a meal attached.

movements so clumsy and comical that they became the source of the word "buffoon." True toads are generally brown or tan. In contrast, members of the genus *Atelopus,* the harlequin frogs of Central and South America that also belong to this family, display vivid yellow or red markings on a shiny black background.

Even more colorful are the dendrobatids, the poison frogs of Central and South America. While nearly all anurans have at least a little poison in their skins, some dendrobatids are highly toxic. Secretions from their skin

Most predators avoid the harlequin poison dart frog *(Dendrobates histrionicus)* of South America because its skin contains enough poison to kill a medium-sized monkey. If the toxin enters a human's bloodstream, it damages the central nervous system.

are an ingredient in the poison that some native hunters put on their darts and arrows. It quickly paralyzes or kills their prey. These frogs advertise danger with their coloring: bright gold, blue, green, yellow, or red, sometimes with eye-catching spots or stripes. In contrast, the nontoxic members of the dendrobatid family have cryptic coloration: quiet greens and browns that camouflage them in the forest environment.

Two species of parsley frogs exist. One is widely distributed across Spain, France, and Portugal. The other lives between the Black and Caspian seas in western Asia. Both are covered with green speckles, spend most of their time on land, and are active at night.

The Mexican burrowing toad, *Rhinophrynus dorsalis,* is the only species in its family. Round and short-legged, it lives underground in burrows that it excavates with tubercles on its hind feet. It lives not just in coastal areas of Mexico but north to the Texas coast and south as far as Costa Rica.

A family of European anurans contains the midwife toads and painted frogs. The toads have plump bodies, short legs, and rough, warty skins. Active at night, they spend the daylight hours in burrows or cool, moist hiding places under rocks or logs. Painted frogs, which are often found in or near shallow water, have slender bodies and long, narrow snouts.

The three species of Seychelles frogs are an example of an anuran family with extremely limited range, or geographic distribution. They are found only on some of the Seychelles, a small cluster of islands in the Indian Ocean. They are terrestrial, and the female lays her eggs not in water but on damp ground. She tends them until they hatch and then the male carries the tadpoles on his back until they have developed into froglets.

The Mexican burrowing toad inflates its body with air to appear larger when it is threatened. It also inflates when uttering its call, which is a loud, low "whoooooa" sound.

Villagers in the African nation of Cameroon weigh a Goliath frog. These anurans, the largest in the world, are a threatened species.

The widest range of any anuran family is that of the Ranidae, or true frogs. With hundreds of species in dozens of genera, this family is found in North, Central, and South America, Africa, Europe, and Asia. A few species even survive north of the Arctic Circle in Russia and Canada. The family of Ranidae includes Indian tree frogs, one of the many groups of anurans that have evolved into an arboreal, or tree-dwelling, way of life. It also contains a number of the world's most common and familiar frogs, such as the American bullfrog, the edible frog, the wood frog, and the European common frog. The world's largest frogs are Ranidae. These are *Conraua goliath,* the Goliath frogs of Africa, which can measure 11.75 inches (30 centimeters) in length (from the nose to the rear of the body, not counting the legs) and weigh 7.25 pounds (3.3 kilograms).

Another family contains the world's tiniest anurans, the Brazilian three-toed toadlets. These little animals live in southeastern Brazil on forest floors, hidden among fallen leaves. The smallest adult on record was about half an inch (12 millimeters) long. (*Pseudacris ocularis,* a grass frog, is roughly the same size, although it belongs to a different family and lives in the southeastern United States.)

The *Brachycephalus* genus of three-toed toadlets (also called saddleback frogs) includes the world's smallest anuran species. It has two common names: Izecksohn's toad and the Brazilian gold frog.

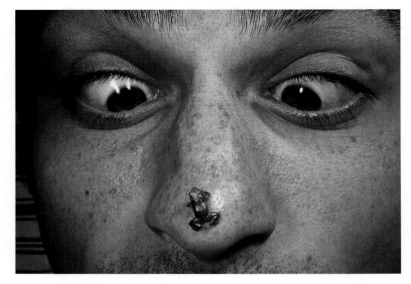

Ghost frogs live in swift-flowing streams in South Africa. Their tadpoles are well suited to survive in fast-moving water, with long, strong tails for swimming in the current and large mouths that they use as suckers to cling to steep rocks, where they graze on algae.

Australian ground frogs live in a variety of habitats in Australia and the neighboring large island of New Guinea. They are found in rain forests, grasslands, and swamps. Some species are adapted to desert life. During dry periods they retreat to burrows, surviving on water they have stored in their bodies. They wait for rainstorms, when they will emerge to seek food and soak up more water.

Parental care varies among anurans. Some species simply lay eggs and leave. In other species, the male or the female carries the young until they are large enough to find food on their own.

Australian toadlets and water frogs live in southern New Guinea and eastern and western Australia. They tend to be plump-bodied, with short legs. Depite the name "water frogs," most species are terrestrial. Like the Australian ground frogs, the toadlets and water frogs occupy a wide range of habitats. Some have distinctive parenting practices. The female hip-pocket frog lays eggs on the ground. When the tadpoles hatch, they squirm into pouches in the skin along the sides of the male's body—these give the species its common name. The tadpoles develop into small adults inside these pouches. In another group, the female lays eggs in a stream, then swallows them. Her stomach stops producing digestive acids, and the eggs develop in her stomach. Young froglets emerge from her mouth six or seven weeks later.

The mouth-brooding frogs of South America have a similar strategy. Females lay their eggs on the ground. Males take care of the eggs for twenty days or so, when they hatch into tadpoles. Then the males gather up the tadpoles in their mouths. One species releases the tadpoles into water, while another keeps the tadpoles in his vocal sac, the inflatable skin pouch under the chin that fills with air when the frogs are calling.

The large family of leptodactylid frogs is native to Central and South America and the islands of the Caribbean. It includes the Lake Titicaca frog, which has adapted to life in a cold, oxygen-poor lake high in the Andes Mountains. This frog's skin is very baggy, increasing the surface area available for cutaneous respiration. Another species, the Puerto Rican live-bearing frog, is one of the few anurans that gives birth to live young rather than laying eggs—unfortunately, it is considered extinct by some researchers. The male white-lipped frog, also native to Puerto Rico, communicates by making sounds like most other anurans, but it also produces seismic waves by thumping its vocal sac on the ground. Other males pick up these vibrations and sense its presence. Some leptodactylids, such as the Brazilian horned toad, have spikes or stiff flaps of skin that look like horns. These are generally large, wide-mouthed animals and are often called toads. Meat-eaters and hunters, they consume small rodents, lizards, and other animal prey.

Glass frogs are small anurans with semi-transparent skin that contains unique pigments. These pigments reflect infrared radiation, just as the leaves of plants do. Scientists think that the frogs' skin helps camouflage them when they are perched on leaves, making them "invisible" to predatory snakes and birds.

Glass frogs live in Central and South America. Their main habitat is cloud forest—dense rain forests high in the mountains that receive a lot of moisture from clouds. Many of these frogs have semi-transparent skin. Generally small, ranging in size from 1.25 to 2.5 inches (3 to 7 cm), glass frogs are arboreal. The tips of their fingers and toes are enlarged to form pads. Special cells on the pads release mucus that helps the frogs stick to vertical surfaces, or even to the undersides of leaves. Arboreal frogs in other families also have adhesive toe pads.

Adhesive toe pads that grip branches make tree frogs excellent climbers and jumpers. Most species are active at night. Big eyes give them good vision even at low light levels.

Closely related to the glass frog—at least in the opinion of some taxonomists—is Ruthven's frog, a little-known species found in 1926 in the rain forest north of the Amazon River. The relationship between Ruthven's frog and other frogs is a mystery, because few specimens have been examined. The first scientist to describe the animal considered it a type of toad because, like some anurans that are commonly called toads, it lacks teeth. More recently, some researchers have identified Ruthven's frog as a member of the glass frog family, while others place it in a family by itself.

A mystery of a different kind gave the paradox frog its name. A paradox is something that seems to contradict itself, and in this case, the paradox is size. Tadpoles of the paradox frog are huge, sometimes 10 inches (25 cm) long, Surprisingly, however, the adult frogs are not correspondingly large—they are only 2.5 inches (6.5 cm) in length. The growth patterns of other members of this family are less startling. All frogs in the family are aquatic.

The hylids, or Amero-Australian tree frogs, are a big family, with around forty genera and nearly eight hundred species. In addition to the Americas and Australia, they are found in Europe and Asia. Most hylids have slender, long-legged bodies and adhesive toe pads. They live in trees and are generally active at night. Green and gray tree frogs and northern cricket frogs are among the hylids found in the United States. The Jamaican snoring frog, one of the world's largest tree frogs, is a hylid that lives in hollow trees on the Caribbean island of Jamaica. Males of this species make loud calls that sound like snores.

The Afro-Asian tree frogs inhabit Africa, southern India, and Southeast Asia. Although a few species live on the ground and are active by day, most live in trees and are nocturnal. They are excellent climbers. Some of them, such as Wallace's flying frog, glide through the air from branch to branch, spreading their legs and using the webbing between their toes like four small parachutes. The mantellas of Madagascar also belong to this family. Like the American dendrobatids, mantellas are brightly colored and highly toxic.

Wallace's flying frog doesn't really fly, but it can glide for up to 50 feet (15 m) from tree to tree. It is named for Alfred Russel Wallace, a nineteenth-century British naturalist who spent years'studying the wildlife of Southeast Asia.

Two families of frogs are found only in Africa south of the Sahara Desert. One family, the squeakers and cricket frogs, lives in damp forests and is noted for its chirping sounds. The other, the shovel-nosed frogs, occupies drier regions. These frogs use their hard, pointed snouts to dig burrows.

Reed and sedge frogs also occur across sub-Saharan Africa, but they are found in Madagascar and the Seychelles as well. Some of these small frogs are arboreal, while others are terrestrial. They vary in appearance. Most are green or brown, but some have bright red, yellow, or orange patterns.

Narrow-mouthed frogs, also called microhylids, live in the American, African, and Asian tropics. Some are tree-climbers with toe pads. Others are small, round-bodied, burrowing frogs that remain underground until

The rainbow burrowing frog, a member of the narrow-mouthed frog or microhylid family, lives in the highlands of south-central Madagascar, off the coast of Africa. This frog is a male—the female's coloring is even brighter.

rain signals the beginning of their mating season. Globular African rain frogs even raise their young underground—the eggs develop first into tadpoles, then into froglets, all in burrows that their parents have dug.

MATING AND METAMORPHOSIS

Frogs have symbolized fertility and reproduction to many cultures. Heqet, the ancient Egyptian goddess of childbirth, had the head of a frog, and pregnant Egyptian women wore small frog images to protect their developing children. A medieval European superstition said that seeing a toad guaranteed a happy marriage. In India, some people still hold ceremonial weddings of frog brides and grooms to encourage rainfall, which makes the land fertile.

Frogs also represent transformation—dramatic change, such as rebirth after death. A Buddhist legend tells how a frog was reborn into a powerful

FROG METAMORPHOSIS

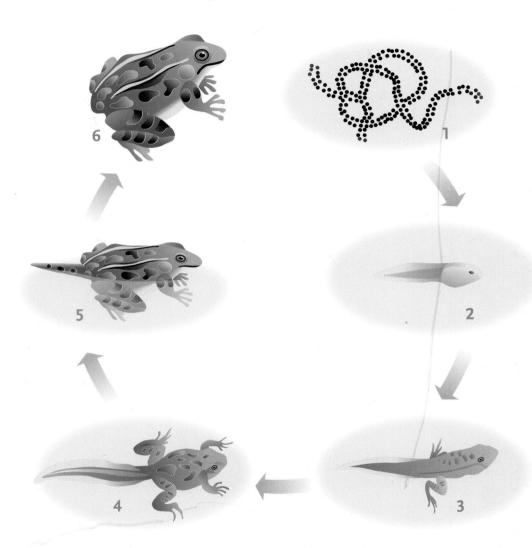

Not all frogs follow the same path to maturity, but many go through these stages. An egg from an egg mass (1) hatches into a tadpole (2). Hind legs develop (3), then front legs (4). In the next stage (5), the tail gets smaller and the animal can breathe air. Metamorphosis ends when the animal becomes a froglet (6), a miniature adult.

god, Indra. In Chinese and Indonesian tales, frogs are magical creatures that gain the ability to fly. And in some well-known transformation tales, a prince or princess is turned into a frog by a wicked enchanter and can become human again only after being kissed.

It's easy to see how frogs became symbols of fertility and transformation. Most species produce very large numbers of eggs. Then, during metamorphosis, the eggs change visibly from eggs to tadpoles to miniature adults.

Anuran reproduction begins with mating. The male frog sits on the female's back and grasps the female behind her head with his forelegs in a

Ponds in eastern North America echo the call of the male spring peeper—a single clear, high note repeated over and over. Frogs call by squeezing their lungs while keeping their mouths and noses shut. This inflates their vocal sacs and passes air across their vocal chords. Calls serve many purposes: attracting mates, marking territory, and warning away possible rivals.

Males and females of the common frog, *Rana temporaria,* gather at ponds called spawning sites to breed. Females lay hundreds of eggs, which may form large masses in the water. After they are fertilized, the eggs rise to the surface.

mating posture called amplexus. Some species stay this way for a few seconds, others for hours or days. In some species, rival males swarm around breeding females, competing with each other for mating rights.

In most cases, the female deposits her eggs and the male then fertilizes them outside her body. Males of some species, however, pass their sperm into their mates' bodies for fertilization. The young of these species may develop inside the mother's body, to be born alive, but the majority of anurans are oviparous, which means that they lay eggs. Like all amphibian eggs, frog eggs lack hard shells, but a protective coating of soft jelly encloses them. Depending upon the species, there may be a single egg or thirty thousand. Laid either in water or on land, the eggs may form long strands or clusters.

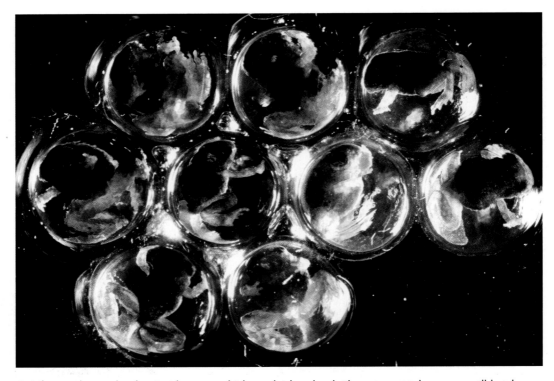

Rainfrog embryos develop inside eggs, which are laid on land. These terrestrial anurans will hatch as tiny froglets without passing through a tadpole stage.

In about 80 percent of all anuran species, the eggs hatch into larval forms called tadpoles. The other 20 percent are terrestrial species that lay their eggs on land; these eggs develop directly into miniature versions of the adult form, without passing through the larval stage.

A newly hatched tadpole has two visible body parts: a head and a tail. Tadpoles move by thrashing their tails and breathe through gills. They are basically free-swimming eating machines. They eat algae, although many species also feed on dead fish and worms, and some—called cannibal tadpoles—eat live prey, including other tadpoles. The young of some species spend years as larvae. Others, such as the spadefoot toads, pass through the larval stage in little more than a week.

As tadpoles grow larger, they begin to acquire the features of the next stage of life. Hind legs appear—or, if they have been present for some time, they grow longer and stronger. The large head begins to take on the form of a body. At metamorphosis, the young animal loses its tail, which is absorbed back into the body, and gains forelegs. Its gills disappear and its lungs begin to function, allowing it to breathe air and leave the water. During this phase, the amphibian is called a metamorph.

Once the tail is gone and the legs and lungs are fully developed, the metamorph is considered a froglet, a young form of the adult it will become—if it is not snapped up by a turtle, bird, fish, or other predator. Metamorphosis may not be as romantic as being kissed by a princess, but it has worked for amphibians for millions of years.

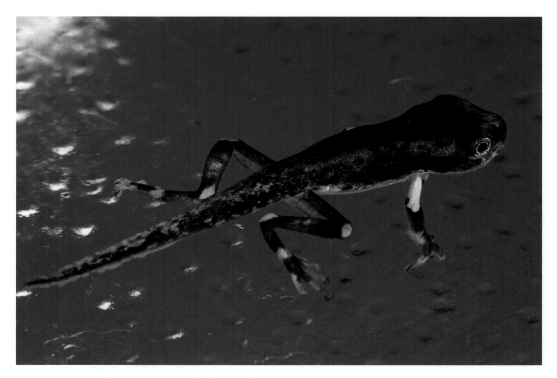

During metamorphosis, a tadpole's limbs develop and its tail shrinks and is absorbed into the body.

A Rare and Remarkable Find

The Western Ghats are mountains in southern India. Once they were heavily forested, but the growing human population in the region has stripped the tree cover from all but about 10 percent of the mountain range. Yet the Ghats still hold some secrets, as scientists Franky Bossuyt and S.D. Biju reported in the magazine *Nature* in 2003. In the Sahyadri region of the Ghats, they discovered a burrowing frog that spends most of its life underground. It proved to be not just a new species, but a very unusual one, and a bit of a taxonomic mystery. Bossuyt and Biju claimed that the frog is so different from all other anurans that it belongs in a completely new family of its own. They gave it the scientific name *Nasikabatrachus* (from words meaning "nose" and "frog") *sahyadrensis.*

Blackish-purple in color, *Nasikabatrachus* is, to put it bluntly, funny-looking. One journalist wrote that "it looks more like a squat, grumpy blob than a living creature." Another compared it to "a bloated doughnut with stubby legs and a pointed snout." But the frog was a thing of beauty to the scientists. Finding a new species is not uncommon, but discovering a whole new family is "a once-in-a-century find," according to evolutionary biologist Blair Hedges of Pennsylvania State University.

Nasikabatrachus's closest relatives, it turns out, are the Seychelles frogs. DNA analysis shows that the ancestors of the two families evolved

Nasikabatrachus is the amphibian treasure of the Western Ghats.

apart some 130 million years ago. Yet the newly discovered frog raises questions. Why did it evolve so long in isolation, when many other frog families span several continents? Does *Nasikabatrachus* have close relatives that have not yet been discovered? Only future finds—perhaps of fossils, perhaps of living frogs—can answer those questions.

The ensatina salamander lives on the West Coast of North America, from British Columbia to Baja, California. Scientists think that it is a single species now splitting up into seven or more related species in different parts of its geographic range.

Salamanders and Newts

Salamanders can live in fire—or so people used to think. Their name comes from the Latin word *salamandra,* or "fire-lizard." In the fourth century BCE the Greek philosopher and scientist Aristotle wrote, "Now the salamander is a clear case in point, to show us that animals do actually exist that fire cannot destroy; for this creature, so the story goes, not only walks through the fire but puts it out in doing so."

Aristotle was wrong. Fires can and do destroy salamanders. Yet there is a grain of truth in the legend. Some salamanders *can* survive very brief exposure to flames. California newts, for example, have been seen to pass quickly through narrow bands of flame during brush fires. When the newts are exposed to dangerous heat, their skins release a protective coating of mucus. The mucus foams and hardens in the fire, but afterward the newts can scrape it off with their feet. Other species may share the California newt's useful ability.

A sixteenth-century image illustrates the old belief that a salamander could survive amid flames. The salamander wears a crown because this was an emblem of the king of France.

WHAT'S NEWT?

There are more than 550 species of salamanders and newts in the Order Caudata, which means "with tails." Unlike anurans, all caudates have tails. They also have long, narrow bodies that, unlike frogs' bodies, are flexible and can bend from side to side. Most caudates are four-legged, but a few types have lost their hind legs. Some species are completely terrestrial, some are completely aquatic, and some are true amphibians who spend time in both worlds.

When it is time for breeding, many species of salamanders and newts return to the spots where they were born. They have been known to migrate over several miles of difficult terrain to reach these sites. They navigate using sight, smell, and other special senses. The pineal gland, located inside the skull, senses polarized sunlight and helps them tell direction.

Scientists think that some species can also detect the earth's magnetic fields, which may help them remember "maps" of their environment.

The reproductive cycle of caudates is similar to that of frogs. Metamorphosis seems less striking, however, because caudates don't change as much as frogs (they keep their tails). In the most common form of caudate mating, the male produces a spermatophore, a gel-covered capsule containing sperm. He then transfers the spermatophore to the female—a maneuver that may involve elaborate courtship rituals, such as waving his tail to blow his pheromones in her direction, or grasping her with his limbs and tail. Depending upon the species, the female may lay

Eurycea longicauda is native to eastern North America. The species name *longicauda* has the same meaning as its common name, the long-tailed salamander.

The larva of a newt can be seen inside this egg.

her eggs on land or in the water. The number of eggs ranges from half a dozen to about five thousand. As with frogs, a few species of caudates give birth to live larvae or tiny, fully metamorphosed young.

One unusual feature of the caudate life cycle is that some individuals in various species keep larval features, such as gills and finlike membranes on their tails, for much longer than usual. Scientists call this phenomenon neoteny. Some neotenic salamanders simply spend an unusually long time

SALAMANDER METAMORPHOSIS

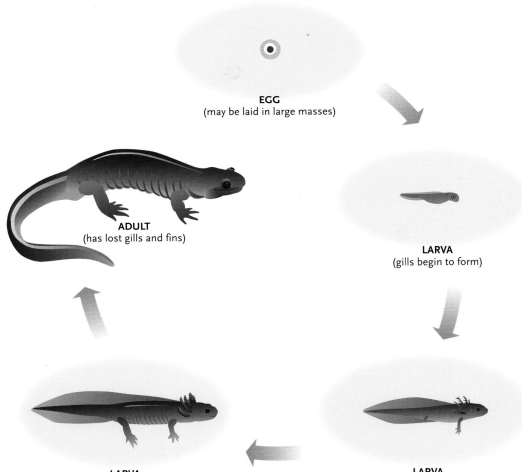

EGG
(may be laid in large masses)

LARVA
(gills begin to form)

LARVA
(has gills, forlegs, and
beginnings of hind legs)

LARVA
(has gills and limbs)

ADULT
(has lost gills and fins)

A salamander's body changes less than a frog's during metamorphosis. Frog tadpoles lose their tails, but salamanders keep them. Not all salamanders go all the way through the cycle. Some of them remain in the larval stage for a long time. Sometimes they even reproduce as larvae and never take on the adult form at all.

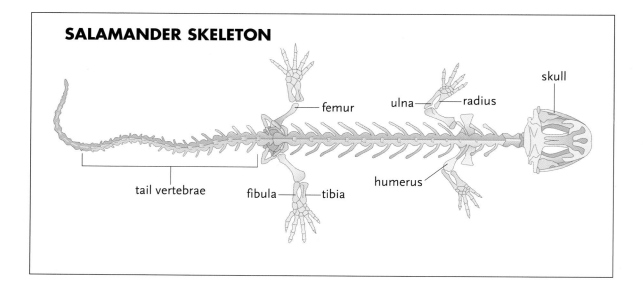

SALAMANDER SKELETON

skull

femur

ulna — radius

tail vertebrae

fibula — tibia

humerus

as larvae. Others never mature past the larval state. Still others reach sexual maturity and can reproduce while they are still larvae. Although scientists know that the animals produce chemicals called hormones that control how they mature, they do not yet understand the reasons for neoteny.

Caudates are less widely distributed than anurans. Nearly all of them live in the northern hemisphere, in climates that are neither extremely hot nor extremely cold. Caudates like humidity. They breathe through their smooth skin, which must be kept moist. For this reason terrestrial species avoid direct sunlight and are often found in caves and burrows, or under rocks and logs. Caudates continue to grow at a slow rate throughout their lives. As a result, all species frequently shed their skin (usually eating the old skin once it has peeled off).

The difference between a salamander and a newt is much like the difference between a frog and a toad. It has more to do with traditional common names than with a scientific distinction. Technically, all caudates are salamanders. The name "newt," though, may be used for varieties that can only breed in water and must return to lakes or ponds for breeding periods each spring.

The feathery growths behind this larval newt's head are its gills. In most caudates, gills disappear after the larval stage, but some salamanders and newts keep them throughout life.

SALAMANDER FAMILIES

The number of families in the Order Caudata varies from one taxonomic system to another, but many experts agree on ten families. Three of these, considered to be the oldest living caudate families, practice external fertilization, in which the female deposits her eggs on leaves or on the ground, and the male fertilizes them outside her body. The remaining caudates practice internal fertilization, in which the sperm passes into the female's body before she lays her eggs.

The sirens are the most ancient family of caudates. Sirens are easy to recognize because they have no hind legs, and their forelegs are tiny. All four species of sirens keep their gills, which look like ferns or feathers behind their eyes, throughout their lives. Instead of teeth, sirens have hard, beaklike biting structures. The largest species, the greater siren, can reach lengths of 36 inches (90 cm), while dwarf sirens range from 4 to 10 inches (10 to 25 cm) in length. Sirens live in shallow muddy or sandy waters in the southeastern United States and northeastern Mexico. They can survive hot, dry spells by entering a state called estivation. When they estivate, mucus covers all parts of their bodies except their mouths, hardening to form a shell; when the water returns, the shell softens and falls away.

Sirens spend most of their time on the bottoms of ponds or streams, but they can wriggle across short stretches of land to get from pool to pool. The lesser siren is unusually vocal for a salamander—it makes clicking sounds and shrill calls.

The giant salamanders are another early caudate family. They are heavily built, with short, thick tails and folds of skin along their sides. All three species live in rivers and feed at night on fish, worms, snails, and other aquatic creatures. The hellbender lives in the eastern United States. The Japanese giant salamander lives in southern Japan. The Chinese giant salamander, sometimes caught and eaten by people in China, is the world's largest species of caudate. The biggest recorded individual was 6 feet (1.8 m) long and weighed 143 pounds (65 kg).

The Asiatic salamanders are the third of the early families. They are distributed across much of Asia, as far north as Siberia. Asiatic salamanders live on land but breed in water, usually fast-moving mountains streams.

The Aztecs dined on axolotls, which they called "water monsters." Although international conservation groups consider the axolotl an endangered species, some people still eat them today.

They have thick bodies and tails. Some species lack lungs and breathe only through their skins.

Mole salamanders, as their name suggests, live underground in burrows. Found in Canada, the United States, and Mexico, these smooth, shiny salamanders are brown or black. They may be spotted or striped with pink, green, yellow, red, blue, orange, or white. One species, the axolotl, is found only in Lake Xochimilco in Mexico. Its name comes from the Aztec words for "water monster." Despite this unappetizing name, the Aztecs ate axolotls, which they considered delicacies. In nature, axolotls never mature past their larval form, although captive axolotls may metamorphose if injected with hormones. Wild axoltls remain aquatic and do not shed their gills.

Pacific mole salamanders live in mountainous areas on the west coast of the United States. They are largely terrestrial, but their anatomy is adapted to the steep, fast-flowing streams in which they breed. These salamanders have small lungs in relation to their body size. This reduces their buoyancy in water, preventing them from being swept away by the current.

Torrent salamanders live in habitats similar to those of the Pacific mole salamanders: the cool, damp forests of the Pacific Northwest. Their larval stage is unusually long, lasting three to five years. Brown-backed and yellow-bellied, torrent salamanders are usually found under rocks in streams, although during periods of heavy rain they move about on the forest floor.

The family of newts and European salamanders is large, diverse, and widely distributed in North America, Europe, and Asia. Many are brightly colored and toxic. Some species are terrestrial, others aquatic. Their typical prey includes worms, insects, slugs, snails, and crayfish. Newts in this family breed in water in the spring, migrating for up to several miles to breed in the same ponds where they were born. Upon returning to their breeding sites, they undergo a kind of reverse metamorphosis. For a short time, they regain some larval features. Their tails become flatter and stronger for better swimming, and their eyes change shape to help them focus underwater. Webbing appears between the toes of males' hind feet so that they can swim fast enough to catch females.

Amphiumas, found in the southeastern United States, are swamp-dwelling caudates with long, tube-shaped bodies and dark, wet skin. They have been mistaken for eels because their legs are so extremely tiny that they can be hard to see. Amphiumas are aquatic, although they sometimes slither across short stretches of land from one body of water to another. They have two defenses against predators—slimy skin that makes them hard to catch, and strong jaws for biting. Like some other amphibians, they estivate during periods of drought, sometimes for as long as three years.

The proteid family includes olms, mudpuppies, and waterdogs. All of these are aquatic salamanders. Mudpuppies and waterdogs, which live in

Their toes are almost impossible to see, but this amphiuma has three on each of its small feet. Both the three-toed and the two-toed species of amphiuma have been known to reach 39 inches (100 cm) in length.

the eastern United States, got their names because people thought that their calls sounded like dogs barking. They are thick-bodied and gray or brown in color, with long, plumelike gills. The slim, ghostly pale olm is one of the least-known caudates. It lives in cave rivers in Italy and Slovenia, on the coast of Europe's Adriatic Sea. The first recorded sighting of this rare, secretive amphibian took place in 1744 when a flood swept one out of its underground habitat. Its discoverer thought that it was a baby dragon.

A mudpuppy is at home in a waterway in the eastern United States. The dark mass of tissue behind its head is its gills.

The lungless salamanders are the largest caudate family, with about 375 species. As their name suggests, they have no lungs. All breathing is done through the skin on their bodies and inside their mouths. Because lungless salamanders need to stay moist, terrestrial species that live in climates with dry seasons—such as the eastern half of the United States—must spend a lot of time estivating, or at least lying low in damp crevices. Some lungless salamanders, however, have moved south into the tropical rain forest of Central and South America, where they remain active all year. Some species have become arboreal. An example of amphibian adaptability, they have developed the ability to grasp tree branches with their tails, something no other salamander can do.

A lungless tree salamander, one of the handful of caudate species that have adapted to life in the trees.

Can This Salamander Be Saved?

The Siskiyou Mountains straddle the border between southern Oregon and northern California. This rocky, heavily forested region is home to the Siskiyou Mountain salamander, *Plethodon stormi.* Brown with white speckles, about 4 inches (10 cm) long, the salamander spends a lot of time underground, emerging in spring and fall to feed on insects and worms.

The California Endangered Species Act (CESA) lists the Siskiyou Mountain salamander as a threatened species. This means that some areas of the salamander's habitat are protected by law, although the state's Department of Fish and Game (DFG) has suggested removing the salamander's threatened status and stripping it of protection, over the objections of wildlife biologists and environmentalists.

In May 2005, researchers led by a U.S. Forest Service biologist published the results of their genetic study of some salamanders collected from an area called Scott Bar, where the Scott and Klamath rivers meet in northern California. The salamanders from Scott Bar had wider heads, longer legs, and shorter tails than usual. They were so different from the main population of Siskiyou Mountain salamanders, said the researchers, that they formed an entirely new species—*Plethodon asupak* (Asupak is the Shasta Indian name for Scott Bar).

Finding a new salamander is a reason for biologists to celebrate. "This is really an exciting discovery," said Joseph Vaile of the Klamath-Siskiyou Wildlands Center. The discovery, however, could have tragic results for the newly identified species.

After the researchers made their announcement, the DFG claimed that because the animals were no longer considered to be Siskiyou Mountain

Scott Bar salamanders

salamanders—and because the Scott Bar salamander *wasn't* on the CESA list—their habitat did not have to be protected. The DFG declared that Scott Bar salamander's only known habitat could be logged. This would pose a serious threat to the survival of the salamander, which needs heavy forest cover to maintain the cool, damp conditions it needs.

Conservation groups have filed several lawsuits in California state court, hoping to force the DGF to protect both Scott Bar and Siskiyou Mountain salamanders. "We are just beginning to understand these unique salamanders that breathe through their skin and primarily live under the cover of old-growth forests," said Lindsey Holme of the Environmental Protection Information Center (EPIC). "Yet the Department of Fish and Game is rushing their habitat to the chopping block."

The Scott Bar salamander's numbers are unknown, like much else about it. Scientists think the salamander may have lived in the Siskiyous since before the last Ice Age, which ended some ten thousand years ago. Soon, though, this species' fate may be decided in a courtroom.

The sticky caecilian, *Ichthyophis glutinosus,* belongs to one of the two oldest families of caecilians.

Caecilians

The number of people in the world who study caecilians, said journalist Kathryn Phillips in her 1994 book *Tracking the Vanishing Frogs,* "could probably fit into a standard-size hot tub." Caecilians are challenging to observe and may be fairly rare in some parts of their range. They are the least-known order of amphibians.

Most people will never see a caecilian. Those who do see one may mistake it for an earthworm. Caecilians' bodies, like those of earthworms, are tube-shaped and covered with skin that forms narrow rings or segments called annuli. And like earthworms, caecilians spend nearly all of their time underground. Terrestrial species excavate tunnels. Aquatic species burrow into the bottoms of lakes or streams.

E V O L U T I O N   A T   W O R K

Caecilian anatomy differs from batrachian anatomy in several ways. Unlike the other two orders of amphibians, caecilians have scales, at least in some species. The scales are small, covered by the skin folds of the

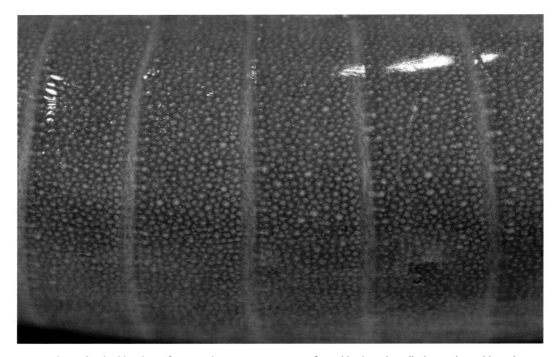

A caecilian's body, like that of an earthworm, is a series of ringlike bands called annuli. Unlike other amphibians, some caecilians have small flat scales that can be seen when the skin between the annulia is stretched out.

annuli. They resemble fish scales rather than reptile scales. Comparisons of the various caecilian families show that the order is gradually losing its scales. The two families that taxonomists call basal—meaning that they are older and more closely related to ancestral forms—have more scales than the families that later developed from them.

Eocaecilian, the ancestral species known from 190-million-year-old fossils, had small but definite legs. Somewhere along the evolutionary line, though, modern caecilians lost their legs. Other changes adapted caecilians to a life of burrowing. Their skulls became thick, their snouts became more pointed, their mouths moved to the undersides of their heads, and they developed extra muscles to keep their jaws shut. All of these modifications produced heads that could more efficiently ram through soil and mud. These changes are more advanced in the recently developed families of caecilians than in the basal families.

The name "caecilian" comes from the Latin word for blindness. Over time the eyes of caecilians became small and weak because they are not needed in the dark. In some species, the eyes are covered by skin, or even bone. Yet scientists believe that all species of caecilians still have optic nerves, which means that they may still be able to sense light. Caecilians have also developed new sensory organs found in no other amphibians. A caecilian can extend a small, short tentacle from either side of its head. These organs pick up chemical signals from the environment, functioning like a combination of smell and taste.

Gymnophis multiplicata, a caecilian found in the rain forest of Costa Rica, has no eyes. But scientists believe its optic nerve could still function, allowing the caecilian to tell the difference between light and dark.

A caecilian's chemical sensors, possibly combined with an ability to feel earth vibrations caused by movements, help the animal catch its prey. Some caecilians hunt, poking through mud and soil. Most use a "sit and wait" strategy, snatching prey that comes within their grasp and clamping down on it with their strong jaws. Typical food items are worms, termites, crickets, beetles, and small lizards and frogs. Caecilians themselves are eaten by snakes and birds, although poison glands in their skin give them some protection.

All known species of caecilians reproduce through internal fertilization. In egg-laying species, the females tend the eggs, which hatch into larvae that will metamorphose into adults. Other species are viviparous, which means that the females give birth to live young. These young are born after metamorphosis.

The Asiatic yellow-striped caecilian.

Caecilians are found only in tropical and subtropical climates. They appear to be fairly common in southern China and parts of West Africa and Central and South America. They are less often seen in other parts of their known range, but scientists don't know whether this means they are truly rare or just easy to overlook.

CAECILIAN FAMILIES

Caecilians belong to the Order Gymnophiona (or Apoda, which means "without feet"). Some taxonomists group them into as few as three families, but many recognize six families. More than 170 species have been

This caecilian has short tentacles toward the front of its face. These organs, unique to caecilians, may help the animals "see" by picking up chemical cues in their subterranean environments.

Dermophis mexicanus, found in Mexico and Central America, may look like an earthworm, but this caecilian's favorite food is earthworms.

identified. Unlike most anurans and caudates, caecilians generally do not have common names, for the simple reason that most people don't even know they exist.

The two basal families are the rhinatrematids, found in northern South America, and the icthyopiids of India and Southeast Asia. These families have features that, herpetologists believe, were present in the ancestral caecilians. Among these features are multiple rings or folds in each body segment, tails that extend past the animals' anuses, and egg-laying reproduction. Larvae breathe through gills and are aquatic, living in streams. After metamorphosis, the adults take up terrestrial life.

The uraeotyphlid family represents a transition between basal and more developed forms of caecilians. Uraeotyphlids live in India. They have short tails and double segment rings, but they also have the skull and jaw adaptations seen in the later families. The uraeotyphlids are the smallest family of caecilians, with one known genus and four species.

Typhlonectids are aquatic or semi-aquatic. Unlike other caecilians, they have a dorsal fin, a ridge that runs along the top of the body, which helps them swim. Their eyes are more functional than those of most caecilians, and their tentacles are small. The range of the typhlonectids covers much of northern South Africa.

Scolecomorphids are a family of caecilians native to the equatorial region of Africa. They have large tentacles on the undersides of their jaws. A unique feature of this family is that the small, almost useless eyes are

The pink-headed dwarf caecilian is one of the smallest species in this order of amphibians. This specimen is from Ecuador.

Many aspects of caecilian biology and life remain mysterious. Scientists hope to answer some puzzling questions about these obscure amphibians before the animals are driven to extinction.

positioned at the base of the tentacles. When a scolecomorphid withdraws its tentacles into its body, the eyes are hidden under the bones of the skull. They reappear when the animal extends its tentacles again.

The largest and most diverse family is the caeciliids, which occur in Central and South America, Africa, India, and the Seychelles Islands. One of the better-known species, represented in some zoo collections, is *Siphonops annulatus,* which has white or light blue rings on a dark blue background. The caeciliid family includes the smallest and the largest members of the order. *Grandisonia brevis*, found in the Seychelles, averages little more than 4 inches (100 mm) in length. South America's *Caecilia thomsoni* can reach lengths of 5 feet (152 cm). Caeciliids' reproductive methods are diverse, too. Some species lay aquatic eggs; others are viviparous. A few species, such as *Afrocaecilia taitana*, lay eggs on land that hatch into young, metamorphosed adults without spending a larval stage in water. As in all caecilian families, many species are known only from one or two examples.

Caecilians—possibly including species not yet discovered—are an unexplored frontier in amphibian biology. That frontier may never be fully explored. Biologist Marvalee H. Wake of the University of California at Berkeley has written, "It is most unfortunate that caecilians are dying, and perhaps even becoming extinct, just as scientists are beginning to appreciate their biology and their place in ecosystems." Caecilians are not the only amphibians in danger. As herpetologists and wildlife biologists have warned many times in recent years, this class of animals now faces an array of threats.

Amphibian species such as this newt, which is native to the foothills of Asia's Himalaya Mountains, are at risk around the world because of habitat loss, pollution, disease, and overharvesting.

Sounding The Amphibian Alarm

We live in a golden age of amphibian discoveries. AmphibiaWeb, a database for information about frogs, salamanders, and caecilians around the world, reported a total of 6,074 species—88 percent anuran, 9 percent caudate, and 3 percent caecilian—in the fall of 2006. Since 1985, the total number of known species had increased by almost 35 percent.

Yet some experts are worried that amphibian species could soon start disappearing in even greater numbers. In 2004, the World Conservation Union (IUCN) and two other international conservation organizations reported the results of a three-year study called the Global Amphibian Assessment (GAA). Five hundred scientists in more than sixty nations analyzed every known amphibian species. Their goal was to estimate the population and range of each species, whenever possible, and to determine whether the species was threatened with extinction.

Their findings were grim. Nearly a third of the world's amphibian species—32 percent—were threatened with extinction (compared with 12 percent for birds and 23 percent for mammals). At least nine species had become extinct since 1980. Another 113 were missing, possibly

The tomato frog, native to Madagascar, is threatened with extinction. The two biggest reasons for the decline in wild tomato frog populations are deforestation and collecting for the pet trade.

extinct. Population numbers were falling in at least 43 percent of species. Amphibians, the scientists confirmed, are in serious trouble.

That may be bad news for other kinds of living things. Amphibians are what ecologists call bio-indicators. Their condition indicates the overall state of the ecosystem where they live. Amphibians make excellent bio-indicators because they are extremely sensitive to changes in the environment. Their permeable, unshielded skin exposes them to water, soil, and sunlight. Small changes in moisture, soil and water chemistry, temperature, and other factors can have a big effect on amphibians.

What's causing the amphibians' decline? One problem is habitat destruction. Many species are so precisely adapted to life in a particular habitat that they cannot survive when their habitat changes. Human activities such as logging, agriculture, and clearing wetlands and forests for construction are likely to disturb any resident amphibians. Mosquito-control measures, such as filling in drainage ditches and ponds, eliminate amphibian habitat. Road-building may break up amphibian populations, making it harder for individuals to reach mates and breeding sites. It also leads to high rates of traffic deaths. Communities in England, Europe, and other places have begun building "toad tunnels" that give amphibians a chance to cross streets and highways without being squashed.

Habitat loss is especially damaging to species with very limited ranges. The Kihansi spray toad of Tanzania, in East Africa, is such a species—it lives only in and around a single waterfall. In recent years the toads have disappeared, perhaps because a new dam upstream greatly lowered the amount of water spray in the air around the waterfall. Two steps have been taken to try to save the Kihansi spray toad: an artificial sprinker system at the waterfall, and a captive breeding program. Scientists hope to breed toads that can be released into the restored habitat.

"Toad tunnels" offer amphibians safe passage under busy streets on their way to breeding grounds. It is too soon to tell whether the tunnels are helping species survive.

The Curse of the Cane Toad

A plump, hardy amphibian known as *Bufo marinus*—the cane toad or marine toad—has taught Australians a hard lesson about the dangers of bringing home a foreign species. Knee deep in toxic toads, the Australians agree with the World Conservation Union, which calls *B. marinus* one of the world's hundred worst plant and animal invaders.

In the early 1930s, sugar planters in the Australian state of Queensland were losing crops to destructive cane beetles. They heard that sugar planters in the Caribbean were solving that problem by importing *B. marinus* from its native South America. The Australians decided to try it. In 1935, over the protests of scientists who warned of possible risks, they released three thousand cane toads into the fields. More releases followed.

The result was an ecological disaster. First, the toads failed to solve the problem. The troublesome beetles spend most of their time in the upper parts of the cane plants, and the toads can't jump high enough to reach them. Second, the toads multiplied like mad in their new environment without natural predators. Third, the invading toads caused trouble—attacking native species, ruining habitats, even killing pets.

What makes cane toads such a menace? For one thing, they are big breeders. A single female can lay 30,000 to 35,000 eggs, more than any other anuran. For another, cane toads poison the native crocodiles, snakes, lizards, and other creatures that try to eat them. The toads are so toxic that dead snakes have been found with toads in their mouths, unswallowed because the snakes died instantly. Toad toxin can poison the water in ponds, pets' drinking dishes, and the watering stations that ranchers keep for their livestock. Veterinarians have reported deaths among dogs that have come into contact with the poisonous amphibians. Some businesses have created toad-proof swimming pools.

Cane toads are voracious eaters. In addition to consuming food that would otherwise be available to native species, they are eating honeybees (causing problems for the beekeeping industry) and other beneficial insects, birds' eggs—and amphibians. Tragically, an introduced amphibian now threatens Australia's native frogs.

The toads have spread across much of Queensland and the neighboring Northern Territory. They have also established themselves in and around Sydney, Australia's major city. Residents of Western Australia are bracing for the arrival of the toads, which are expected to reach their state between 2007 and 2012.

Australians have tried to get rid of the unwanted toads. Some approaches are brutal but simple. In 2005, for example, a member of the government urged citizens to whack toads with golf clubs. Many people have suggested building an enormous fence across the continent, to keep the toads from speading to new areas, but it would be nearly impossible to prevent eggs and tadpoles from traveling along streams and ditches. Researchers have considered attacking the toads with a tailored virus or some other kind of germ warfare, although this method—like the original introduction of the toads themselves—might have drastic, unforeseen effects.

Another approach is finding native species that can strike back at the toads. A promising candidate is the lavender beetle. Some cane toads that eat this beetle die. And one or two Australian snake species seem able to eat the toads without being poisoned. Perhaps they will play a role in exterminating the pests. In the meantime, several native species of rats and birds have learned to eat only the toads' legs and bellies, avoiding the poison on the back and neck.

Cane toads have cost Australians millions of dollars. Programs now underway to control them, and to protect native species threatened by the toads, will cost millions more. The cane toad crisis shows how easily people can upset the balance of nature, even with the best intentions.

Introduced species can put pressure on native amphibians. Trout have been introduced into many lakes in the United States as food and sport fish. Unfortunately for frogs, trout love tadpoles. Sometimes, though, the introduced species is another amphibian. Bullfrogs raised for food in places where they don't naturally occur can destroy populations of native frogs if they escape.

People take amphibians out of their natural habitats for all kinds of reasons. Frogs and toads are hunted for their skins, which can be made into leather. Some kinds of frogs and salamanders are food items in various countries. Traditional folk medicines in China, Mexico, and other nations contain powders made from the dried secretions of toad or

This Tam Dao newt, an endangered species, is being illegally sold in a pet store in Vietnam. The taking of animals from their natural habitats is harming many amphibians species. The Tam Dao newt lives in a specific area. If it disappears from there, it is gone from the wild.

A deformed northern leopard frog. Students' discovery of growing numbers of such frogs kicked off an amphibian alarm.

frog skins and glands. Modern medicine, has also found uses for amphibians' secretions. Chemicals that protect African clawed frogs from bacteria and fungi, for example, are an ingredient in an antibiotic cream used to treat skin ulcers. Cancer patients may take painkillers containing compounds from a South American poison frog. Finally, too many wild amphibians are "harvested" each year for the pet trade. Interest in amphibians is a wonderful thing, but pet owners should buy only animals raised in captivity.

Pollution of the water and air harms amphibians. Fertilizers and pesticides used in agriculture, auto exhaust and oil washed off roadways, househould waste, sewage, and chemical discharges from mines and factories get into the water and the air—and, because of amphibians'

These Hungarian girls are part of a "toad patrol." They are releasing common toads rescued from a busy road.

permeable skin, what gets into the water and the air also gets into the amphibians. Many scientists suspect that toxic pollution is to blame for some disturbing amphibian distress stories. In the 1990s, schoolchildren in Minnesota began finding large numbers of deformed frogs. Alarmed, scientists started examining frog populations there and elsewhere. They found higher-than-normal cases of deformities: frogs with extra legs, useless legs, or no legs at all, and frogs with defective reproductive systems. Experts have not yet pinpointed a specific cause for these malformations and deformities. Many think that the explanation lies in synergy—a number of things working together. The effects of synergy can be subtle, complex, and difficult to untangle.

In addition to various kinds of pollution, the synergy of amphibian declines could involve such factors as rising temperatures (because of global warming) and increased ultraviolet radiation (because pollution has led to a loss of protective ozone in earth's atmosphere). Perhaps no single factor would be enough to kill a frog, salamander, or caecilian. Acting together, though, the factors multiply each other's effects. For example, researchers know that immune systems are often weakened in amphibians and other animals who experience environmental stress. This may be why amphibians worldwide are dying in extraordinary numbers from disease.

The most destructive disease is chytridiomycosis, a fungal infection that is highly contagious. It is spreading through populations in the Americas and Australia, and it has appeared in Europe, Asia, and Africa as well. Evidence suggests that chytridiomycosis is the cause of at least some recent amphibian extinctions. The origins of this disease are unknown. Scientists do not yet know whether it is a new disease, a new form of an older disease, or perhaps a disease that has suddenly become more deadly because amphibian resistance has been weakened in some way.

Around the world, scientists and conservation groups—including grass-roots community organizations that work to protect ponds or parks from development or pollution—are fighting to save endangered amphibians. Through captive breeding programs, efforts to remove introduced species, and projects to restore habitat, they are trying to give frogs, salamanders, and even the usually invisible caecilians a second chance. The Declining Amphibian Populations Task Force (DAPTF), established in 1990 by the IUCN and several national governments, shares information about these efforts and about new research on chytridiomycosis and other threats.

The well-being of amphibians matters to everyone—or should. Amphibian declines "may indicate environmental deterioration that otherwise would not be visible," wrote the authors of the GAA report. "Some scientists believe that the subtle environmental changes created by global

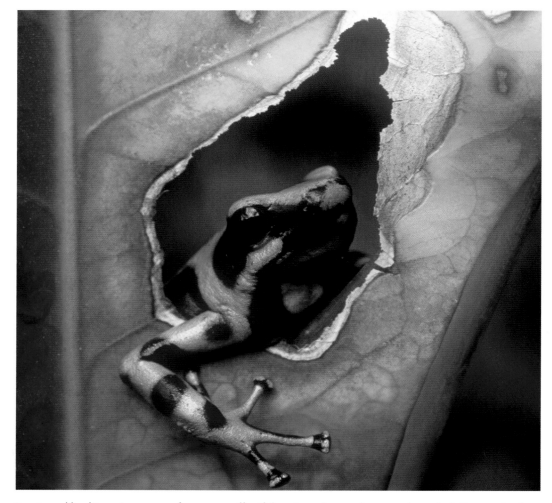

Creatures like this poison arrow frog may suffer if the air and water become degraded. Some scientists think that amphibians' problems are signs of environmental issues that concern us all.

warming could be contributing to these mysterious die-offs, with sensitive amphibian species suggesting the fate of other forms of life." Whatever we do to conserve the amphibians, those living links to the ancient creatures who made homes of both water and land, benefits us all.

adapt—To change or develop in ways that aid survival in the environment.

algae—A one-celled or multicelled plantlike organism generally found in water; usually classified in kingdom of protists, or protozoa.

anatomy—The physical structure of a living organism.

ancestral—Having to do with lines of descent or earlier forms.

anuran—A member of the Order Anura, which includes frogs and toads.

aquatic—Inhabiting water.

arboreal—Living in trees.

batrachian—Having to do with frogs, toads, salamanders, and newts.

conservation—Actions or movements aimed at protecting and preserving wildlife or its habitat.

cutaneous respiration—Breathing through the skin.

ectothermic—Cold-blooded organisms that depend on heat sources outside the body.

evolution—The process by which new species, or types of plants and animals, develop from old ones over time.

evolve—To change over time.

extinct—No longer existing; died out.

genetic—Having to do with genes, material made of DNA inside the cells of living organisms. Genes carry information about inherited characteristics from parents to offspring and determine the form of each organism.

herpetology—The scientific study of amphibians and reptiles.

marine—Inhabiting the ocean.

microscopic—Extremely small; seen clearly (or at all) only through a microscope.

organism—Any living thing.

paleontology—The study of ancient life, mainly through fossils.

pesticide—Something that kills pests.

taxonomy—The scientific system for classifying living things, grouping them in categories according to similarities and differences, and naming them.

terrestrial—Inhabiting land.

vertebrate—An animal with a backbone.

CAUDATA (salamanders and newts)

<u>FAMILIES</u>

Sirenidae (Sirens)
Cryptobranchidae (Giant salamanders)
Hynobiidae (Asiatic salamanders)
Dicamptodontidae (Pacific mole salamanders)
Ambystomatidae (Mole salamanders)
Salamandridae (Newts and European salamanders)
Proteidae (Olms, mudpuppies, waterdogs)
Rhyacotritonidae (Torrent salamanders)
Plethodontidae (Lungless salamanders)
Amphiumidae (Amphiumas)

FAMILY TREE

CLASS AMPHIBIA
3 orders

ANURA (frogs and toads)

GYMNOPHIONA (caecilians)

<u>FAMILIES</u>

<u>FAMILIES</u>

Allophrynidae (Ruthven's frog)
Artholeptidae (Squeakers and cricket frogs)
Ascaphidae (Tailed frogs)
Bombinatoridae (Fire-bellied toads and barbourulas)
Brachycephalidae (Three-toed toadlets)
Bufonidae (True toads and harlequin frogs)
Centrolenidae (Glass frogs)
Dendrobatidae (Poison frogs)
Discoglossidae (Midwife toads and painted frogs)
Heleophrynidae (Ghost frogs)
Hemisotidae (Shovel-nosed frogs)
Hylidae (Amero-Australian tree frogs)
Hyperoliidae (Reed and sedge frogs)
Leiopelmatidae (New Zealand frogs)
Leptodactylidae (Leptodactylid frogs)
Lymnodynastidae (Australian ground frogs)
Megophryidae (Asian toadfrogs)
Microhylidae (Narrow-mouthed frogs)
Myobatrachidae (Australian toadlets and water frogs)
Pelobatidae (Spadefoot toads)
Pelodytidae (Parsley frogs)
Pipidae (Clawed frogs and Surinam toads)
Pseudidae (Paradox frogs)
Ranidae (True frogs)
Rhacophoridae (Afro-Asian tree frogs)
Rhinodermatidae (Mouth-brooding frogs)
Rhinophrynidae (Mexican burrowing toad)
Sooglossidae (Seychelles frogs)

Rhinatrematidae
Ichthyophiidae
Uraetyphlidae
Scolecomorphidae
Typhlonectidae
Caeciliidae

89

F I N D   O U T   M O R E

F U R T H E R   R E A D I N G

Badger, David. *Frogs.* Stillwater, MN: Voyageur Press, 1995.

Beltz, Ellis. *Frogs: Inside Their Remarkable World.* Buffalo, NY: Firefly Books, 2005.

Berger, Melvin. *How Do Frogs Swallow with Their Eyes? Questions and Answers about Amphibians.* New York: Scholastic, 2002.

Cleave, Andrew. *Frogs: A Portrait of the Animal World.* New York: TODTRI, 1999.

Crump, Marty. *Amphibians, Reptiles, and Their Conservation.* North Haven, CT: Linnet Books, 2002.

Discovery Channel Reptiles and Amphibians. New York: Discovery Books, 2000.

Fridell, Ron. *Amphibians in Danger: A Worldwide Warning.* New York: Franklin Watts, 1999.

Gilpin, Daniel. *Tree Frogs, Mud Puppies, and Other Amphibians.* Minneapolis: Compass Point Books, 2006.

Greenberg, Daniel A. *Frogs.* Tarrytown, NY: Benchmark Books, 2001.

Halliday, Tim and Kraig Adler, editors. *Firefly Encyclopedia of Reptiles and Amphibians.* Toronto: Firefly Books, 2002.

Hofrichter, Robert, editor. *Amphibians: The World of Frogs, Toads, Salamanders, and Newts.* Buffalo, NY: Firefly Books, 2000.

Parker, Edward. *Reptiles and Amphibians.* Austin, TX: Raintree Steck-Vaughn, 2003.

Stewart, Melissa. *Amphibians.* New York: Children's Press, 2001.

www.amphibiaweb.org
Amphibia Web, a site inspired by the worldwide drop in amphibian populations, contains information about biology and conservation, as well as an up-to-date count of known amphibian species.

www.open.ac.uk/dapft
The Declining Amphibian Population Task Force of the World Conservation Union maintains this page, with information about amphibian declines, why they matter, and what is being done.

www.frogs.org
The Amphibian Conservation Alliance's site has information about the plight of frogs and other amphibians and plans to protect them.

www.npwrc.usgs.gov/resource/herps/amphibid/
This checklist and idenfitication guide for amphibian species in the United States and Canada is maintained by the Northern Prairie Wildlife Research Center, part of the U.S. Geological Survey.

www.livingunderworld.org/caudata
This site is devoted to salamanders, newts, waterdogs, sirens, mudpuppies, and other amphibians in the order Caudata. It includes a photo gallery, information on caudate biology, and links to other sites.

www.sandiegozoo.org/animalbytes/t-caecilian
The San Diego Zoo's Animal Bytes site offers a quick but informative overview of caecilians, the least-known order of amphibians.

BIBLIOGRAPHY

The author found these books especially helpful when researching this volume.

Clack, Jennifer. *Gaining Ground: The Origin and Evolution of Tetrapods.* Bloomington: Indiana University Press, 2002.

Crump, Martha L. *In Search of the Golden Frog.* Chicago: University of Chicago Press, 2000.

Duellman, William E. and Linda Trueb. *Biology of Amphibians.* Baltimore: Johns Hopkins University Press, 1986.

Mattison, Chris. *Encyclopedia of North American Reptiles and Amphibians.* San Diego: Thunder Bay Press, 2005.

Miller, Gordon L., editor. *Nature's Fading Chorus: Classic and Contemporary Writing about Amphibians.* Washington, DC: Island Press, 2000.

Pough, F. Harvey, et al. *Herpetology.* Third edition. Upper Saddle River, NJ: Pearson Prentice Hall, 2004.

Semlitsch, David, editor. *Amphibian Conservation.* Washington, DC: Smithsonian Books, 2003.

Souder, William. *A Plague of Frogs: The Horrifying True Story.* New York: Hyperion, 2000.

Stebbins, Robert C. *A Natural History of Amphibians.* Princeton, NJ: Princeton Univeristy Press, 1995.

I N D E X

Page numbers in **boldface** are illustrations.

A B O U T   T H E   A U T H O R

Rebecca Stefoff is the author of a number of books on scientific subjects for young readers. She has explored the world of plants and animals in Marshall Cavendish's Living Things series and in several volumes of the AnimalWays series, also published by Marshall Cavendish. For the Family Trees series, she has authored books on primates and flowering plants. Stefoff has also written about evolution in *Charles Darwin and the Evolution Revolution* (Oxford University Press, 1996), and she appeared in the *A&E Biography* program on Darwin and his work. Stefoff lives in Portland, Oregon. You can learn more about her and her books at www.rebeccastefoff.com.